LOOKING AT CHRISTIANITY

Worship

GRAHAM OWEN and ALISON SEAMAN

WAYLAND

LOOKING AT CHRISTIANITY

Festivals
Jesus and Mary
Special Occasions
Worship

Editors: Carron Brown and Ruth Raudsepp
Series consultant: Alison Seaman
Designer and typesetter: Jean Wheeler
Cover designer: Steve Wheele Design
Picture researcher: Gina Brown

First published in 1998 by Wayland Publishers Ltd,
61 Western Road, Hove, East Sussex, BN3 1JD

Find Wayland on the Internet at http://www.wayland.co.uk

British Library Cataloguing in Publication Data
   Seaman, Alison
   Worship. - (Looking at Christianity)
   1. Worship - Juvenile literature
   I.Title II. Owen, Graham
   248.3

ISBN 0 7502 2239 5

Picture acknowledgements
Andes Press Agency/Carlos Reyes-Manzo 27; J. Allan Cash 12; Chapel Studios/Zul Mulchida 23; Greg
Evans 14; Getty Images/Brett Baunton 4; Sonia Halliday 24; Angelo Hornak 25; ICCE/Mark Boulton
19; Topham Picturepoint 17, 18; Trip/B. Seed 13; Wayland Picture Library 20, 22, /Penny Davies 6, 9,
21, 26, /Rupert Horrox 7, 16, /Trevor Hill 10, /Jennie Woodcock 11, 15; Zefa 5, 8.

Cover photo by Danny Allmark.

Printed and bound by EuroGrafica S.p.A., Italy

Contents

All religious words are
explained in the glossary.

 # God's wonderful world

Christians show their wonder at the beauty of God's world.

When Christians worship together, they thank God and try to work with Him to care for the beauty of the world.

Christians believe that God loves everybody.

When they worship together, they remember God's love for the world and for all people.

Saying thank you

Ben says thank you for his present.

Giving and receiving gifts is a way of showing that we love each other. Christians want to say thank you for all God's gifts.

Christians say thank you to God when they meet together.

Annabelle and Jairaj come to church to receive God's gifts of bread and wine from the priest. This is their way of giving thanks to God.

Saying sorry

John and Amy do not always agree with each other.

Sometimes they say things that hurt each other's feelings. John and Amy both think they are right and find it hard to say sorry.

Christians believe it can help to talk about things that have gone wrong.

The priest reminds Angela and Jane that God forgives them for wrongdoing. He helps them to understand how they can make things better.

Being together

The children are making things together and helping each other.

It can be fun to do things together with friends and enjoy each other's company.

When Paresh and Bianca go to church they light candles.

Lighting candles reminds Christians that they are not alone and that God is always there to listen and to help.

Singing praises

John is singing in his church choir.

He practises hard to learn the music. The choir helps everyone to sing praises to God.

Around the world Christians worship God in many different ways.

These Christians in South Africa are singing and dancing outside their church and praising God.

# Praying

Praying brings Christians closer to God.

When Gemma prays, she gets to know God better. Praying helps Gemma to find out what God wants her to do.

These children are talking and listening to God in their prayers.

Some Christians close their eyes when they pray. It helps them to think more carefully about what they are doing.

These children are finding out more about the stories that Jesus told.

Christians learn together by listening to stories from the Bible. They want to know God better and learn about God's love for everyone.

In this picture, a crowd has gathered to see the Pope.

Jesus travelled through towns and villages preaching and teaching. For many Christians today, the Pope is an important leader and teacher. He travels to many towns and countries, preaching about the life of Jesus.

Emma and James are acting out the story of the birth of Jesus.

When Christians worship together at Christmas, they remember the time when Jesus was born in a stable at Bethlehem.

Events in the life of Jesus are told in special plays.

In this play, the actors tell of what happened to Jesus at the end of his life. When Christians worship at Easter, they remember how Jesus was killed in a very cruel way. His hands and feet were nailed to a cross.

Just like us, Jesus enjoyed sharing a meal with his friends and family.

In the Bible, Christians read that when Jesus and his friends met, they ate bread and drank wine. He told them to remember him whenever they ate together.

Christians feel close to Jesus when they share bread.
During their worship, bread is broken and given to everyone. In this way, Christians are doing what Jesus did with his friends.

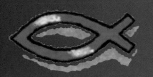

Christians want to worship God in everything they do.

They try to serve God in many different ways. Susan and her mum are serving God by helping their neighbour. They have done some shopping for him.

These children like to go to church with their family and friends every Sunday.

For Christians it is important that they join together to worship God. Sunday is their special day of the week to go to Church.

Going to church

Since the time of Jesus, Christians have made special places for worship.

These places are called churches or chapels. Some churches are very old and people have worshipped there for hundreds of years.

Some churches are richly decorated with pictures.

These pictures help people to understand more about Jesus and the lives of some of his followers.

These children have made a dove like the one on this banner.

The dove is a symbol of God's love for everyone. When Christians worship together, they try to understand how God is still in the world today.

26

These Christians are worshipping God by carrying the cross through their town and showing it to everyone.

Christians believe that Jesus died for them on the cross. They also believe that he came to life again and is with them in all that they do. They are reminded of this every time they worship.

Notes for teachers

About the pictures

The images used in this series are in many respects as important as the text. The historical nature of the subject requires that we use illustrations and photographs as well as actors' representations to enliven the text for children. The images will provide stimuli for discussion and enable children to engage imaginatively with the subject matter.

pp 4–5

Christians believe that God created the world and that they share in the responsibility of caring for it. For some Christians, the descriptions of creation found in the Book of Genesis (chapters 1 & 2) are accepted as a literal account of how the world began. Others would interpret these accounts as attempts to understand the mystery of the origin of the world and humankind. A central Christian belief is that Jesus of Nazareth was a gift from God given in love. In this way, God became human and lived on earth and therefore understands the human condition.

pp 6–7

Pupils will be familiar with the giving and receiving of gifts and the way in which they are encouraged to say thank you. One of the significant reasons for Christians to join together to worship is to say thank you to God. For many Christians, the most important form of worship is the Eucharist, a word that means thanksgiving.

pp 8–9

Pupils will identify with the challenge of human conflict and reconciliation. As teachers and parents, much of your time is spent in resolving disagreements between children. Within Christianity, there is a variety of ways in which guidance is given for the reconciliation of conflict. For some Christians, forgiveness is found through a direct relationship with God. For others, the priest is seen as a confessor, who offers God's pardon for wrong doings.

pp 10–11

Worshipping together helps to reinforce the importance of community life for Christians. Christians also develop their own personal relationship with God through worship. This is expressed in different ways in different Christian communities. For example, some Christians find it helpful to light candles as a way of focusing their attention on God. Others might use words from the Bible, icons or a rosary. For many, however, none of these are considered necessary for worship or to build a personal relationship with God.

pp 12–13

In spite of the diversity of practice in Christian worship, musical expression usually plays a significant role – from the traditional church choir to more informal music making. As a world faith, the music used in Christian worship will often reflect its cultural setting. Hymns, songs and chants are an invaluable teaching resource as they embody much of Christian belief and practice.

pp 14–15

Praying forms a significant part of Christian worship. This is often seen as people conversing with God and by listening, Christians believe they learn what God wants them to do. Well-known Christian prayers are a useful resource for teaching children about Christianity. Christians use familiar set prayers as well as praying using their own words. Traditionally, there is a regular cycle of prayer throughout the day to help Christians to pray.

pp 16–17

The Bible is a sacred text for Christians. It is read by individuals but is also used in public worship. Christians interpret the Bible in different ways but for all Christians, it teaches and guides them in their daily lives. Just as Jesus went about preaching and teaching, so Christians today guide each other in understanding more deeply about the love of God. Significant figures within the Christian community are often looked to for guidance in interpreting scripture.

pp 18–19

The Bible is brought to life through acting out Biblical events. Traditionally, children re-enact the story of the birth of Jesus at Christmas. In medieval times, mystery plays enabled everyone to become familiar with the Bible. This tradition of acting out the story has continued throughout the world in many different settings. Many forms of Church service are a ritual re-enactment of events in the Bible.

pp 20–21

Christian worship takes a variety of different forms and styles. For many Christians, worship is regularly focused on the service known by one of several names – the Eucharist, Mass, Holy Communion or the Lord's Supper. This is a meal which re-enacts the last meal that Jesus shared with his friends before his death. For Christians, it is an opportunity to carry out Jesus' commandment, 'Do this in remembrance of me'.

pp 22–23

Following the example of Jesus, Christians believe they should be of service to others. This can be through their own direct action and by supporting aid organisations that operate throughout the world. Regular worship with other Christians supports both the individual and the world-wide family of the church. When they worship, Christians are reminded to, 'Go in peace to love and serve the Lord'.

pp 24–25

Worship can take place anywhere but traditionally, Christians have created churches as centres for communal worship. Some Christians prefer a simple setting, whilst others enjoy the richness of elaborate buildings. Patterns of worship also range from the informal to the highly ritualistic.

p 26

The idea of God's presence in the world today is often expressed in Christian worship through the symbols of a dove, fire and wind. God's spirit is sometimes seen as a life-giving force which gives life to all living things.

p 27

For Christians throughout the world, the cross is central to Christian worship and a symbol of the life, death and resurrection of Jesus Christ. The name Christ means holy one or anointed one and is used by Christians to identify Jesus as the Son of God.

Glossary

banner A kind of flag, usually made of cloth showing Christian pictures.

Bethlehem The place where Jesus was born.

Bible An important book for Christians.

Christians People who believe in God and God's son Jesus.

Christmas The time when Christians celebrate the birth of Jesus.

Church A building where Christians meet together to worship.

Easter The most important Christian festival, when Jesus died and came back to life.

Jesus Christians believe that Jesus is the Son of God.

Pope An important Christian leader.

prayer When people talk and listen to God.

priest A person who leads worship. They are also called ministers, vicars and pastors.

worship When Christians praise God together.

Books to read

For children

A Child's Book of Prayer in Art by Sister Wendy Beckett
(Dorling Kindesley, 1995)

My Christian Life by Alison Seaman (Wayland, 1996)

The Beginners Bible by Karyn Henley
(Kingsway Publications, 1989)

The Lord's Prayer, retold by Lois Rock, illustrated by
Clare Henley (Lion, 1993)

The World That God Made by Jan Godfrey and Peter Adderley
(A Tamarind Book/SU publishing, 1997)

For teachers

Bridge to Religion, The Warwick Project (Heineman, 1994) –
pupil book, **Lucy's Sunday**, teacher's resource book.

A Gift to the Child, RE in the Primary School by Grimmitt,
Michael Grove, Julie Hull, John Spencer, Louise (Simon Schuster)
– teacher's source book

Index